A New True Book

COMPUTERS

By Karen Jacobsen

This "true book" was prepared
under the direction of
Illa Podendorf,
formerly with the Laboratory School,
University of Chicago

 CHILDRENS PRESS, CHICAGO

Computer terminal

PHOTO CREDITS

Marty Hanson—2, 26, 27 (2 photos), 28, 38 (left), 42

Tony Freeman—4, 35

Harry & Pat Michalski—6, 16, 21 (upper left, lower left), 37 (3 photos)

National Aeronautics & Space Administration: NASA—7, 44

Midway Manufacturing Company—41

Historical Picture Services, Inc.—17, 21 (right), 23

Commonwealth Edison—18

AC Spark Plug Division of General Motors—19

Amana Refrigeration, Inc.—41

Reinhard Brucker—25

Picture Group— ^c Kevin Horan—Cover, 38 (right), ^c Eli Heller, 43

Honeywell Photo Lab—39

Library of Congress Cataloging in Publication Data

Jacobsen, Karen.
    Computers.

    (A New true book)
    Summary: Traces the development of the modern computer from the abacus and early card punch machines, introduces the basic principles of computer technology, and emphasizes the role of computers in our complex society.
    1. Computers—Juvenile literature.
[1. Computers]   I. Title.
QA76.23.J3   001.64   81-38451
ISBN 0-516-01617-2   AACR2

TABLE OF CONTENTS

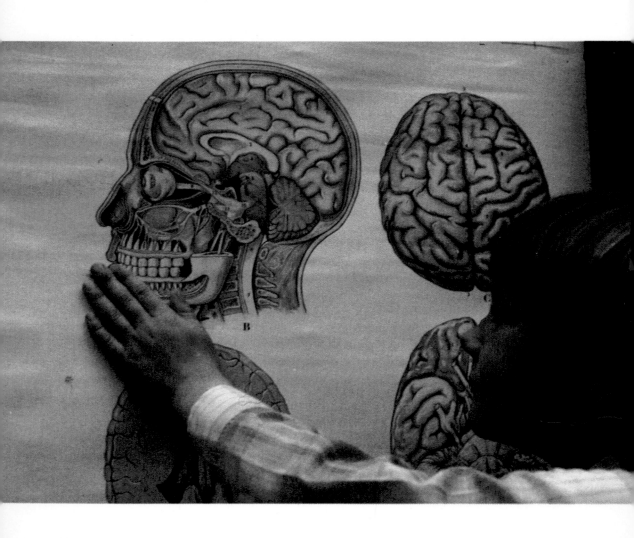

YOU ARE A COMPUTER

Can you count from 1 to 100?

Can you add 21 and 93?

Can you subtract 17 from 68?

If you can do all of these things, then YOU ARE A COMPUTER!

In fact, your brain is the computer. It can count and add and subtract.

Human brain computers are smarter than any other kind of computer. They can have ideas. They can think.

The other computers are machines. They run on electricity. They can do many of the things that human brains can do.

Keypunch operator punches information onto computer cards.

One of the computer rooms at the Johnson Space Center

But machine computers are not intelligent. They cannot think for themselves. They can only think and do what people tell them to think and do.

Computers help people count and keep track of things.

THE FIRST COMPUTERS

From the earliest times people have used their fingers . . . or marks on walls . . . to help themselves remember and count.

One early kind of computer was used for counting. It was probably made of stones.

One stone was equal to one thing.

If a farmer put 40
baskets of grain into the
storehouse, he would get
back 40 special stones.

Each stone was worth
one basket of grain. It
could be traded for
something else or used to
buy back some grain.

Sometime later, someone made a computer.

Three lines were drawn in the sand.

The bottom line was for single numbers—1 to 9.

The second line was for tens—10 to 90.

The third line was for hundreds—100 to 900.

This computer needed only 4 stones to show the number 40.

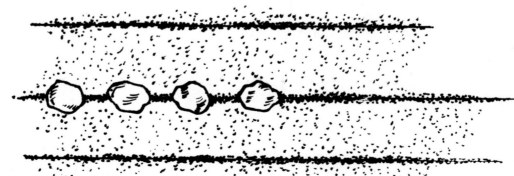

Doing addition is easy on the stone and sand computer.

To add 234 to 40, put 4 stones on the bottom line, add 3 more stones to the 4 stones on the second line, and put 2 stones on the third line. That adds up to 274 of whatever it is that you may be counting.

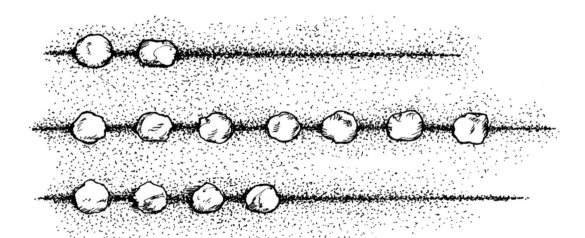

As you can see, 234 + 40= 274.

THE ABACUS

More than 2000 years ago, wood or metal rods replaced the lines drawn in the sand. Beads replaced the stones and a frame surrounded everything.

This simple computer is called an "abacus."

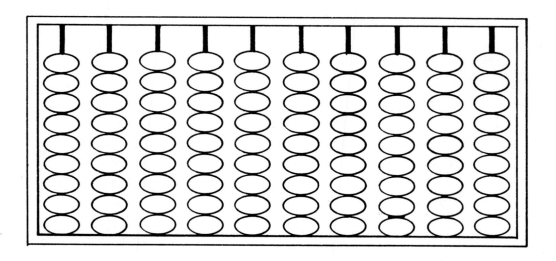

A simple abacus has nine beads on each rod. To show a number, the beads are raised to the top of the frame.

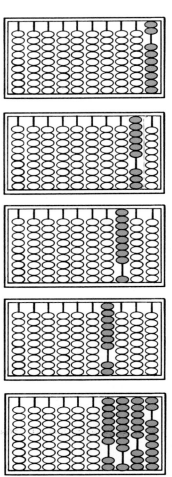

To show the number 2, raise two beads on rod 1.

To show the number 60, raise six beads on rod 2.

To show the number 800, raise eight beads on rod 3.

To show the number 7000, raise seven beads on rod 4.

This abacus shows the number 7862.

An abacus makes addition easy to do.

To add 234 to 7862, start on the right with rod 1.

Add four beads to the two that are already raised.

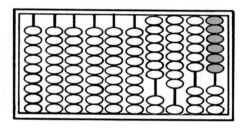

Next, on rod 2, add three beads to the six.

Then, on rod 3, add two beads to the eight.

Oh, no, that won't work. You need ten beads, but there are only nine. Do you know what to do now?

The solution is simple. Put no beads at the top of rod 3. No beads stand for the "0" in the number 10.

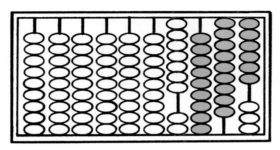

Now, carry the "1" (from the "1" in the number 10) over onto rod 4. Add it to the seven beads that are already there.

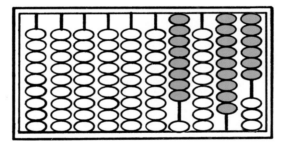

This abacus shows the result of adding 234 to 7862.

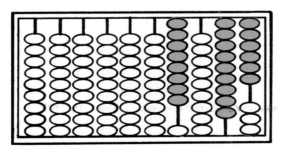

People all over the world use an abacus to solve mathematical problems.

A Chinese abacus has a bar. The two beads above the bar have a value of five. Those below the bar have a value of one. This is how the number 7862 looks on a Chinese abacus.

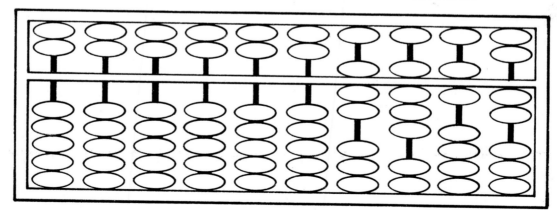

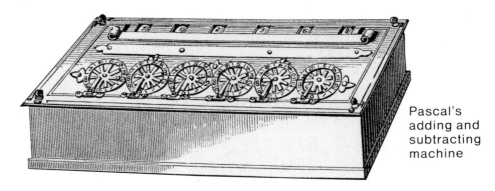

Pascal's adding and subtracting machine

MACHINE COMPUTERS

In 1642, Blaise Pascal, a Frenchman, invented a new kind of computer. It used wheels instead of beads.

Each wheel had ten notches, numbered "0" to "9."

When a wheel was turned seven notches, it added 7 to the total on the machine.

Pascal's machine could add up to 999,999.99. It could also subtract.

The idea of counting with notched wheels is still used today.

Notched wheels in an electric meter box tell how much electricity is used in a building.

Electric meter box

Notched wheels in a mileage meter tell how many miles an automobile travels.

Can you think of other places where wheels are used to count how much or how many?

In the late 1700s in France, Joseph Jacquard invented a way to control the pattern on a loom.

Jacquard punched pattern holes into paper cards. The cards told the loom what to do.

Instead of a person making every change in a pattern, the machine made the changes all by itself.

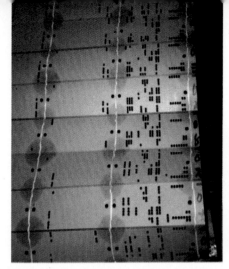

Jacquard's loom (above) used
punched cards (above left) to
control the pattern on a loom (left).

Jacquard's machine
didn't count anything, so it
wasn't a computer. But his
idea led to another
invention.

In 1886, Herman Hollerith, an American, invented a machine to count how many people lived in the United States.

Hollerith used holes punched in cards. The holes stood for facts about a person; such as age, address, or his type of work.

The cards could hold up to 240 pieces of information.

Hollerith's machine ran on electricity.
Tabulating machines (left) and special
punched cards (above) were used to
keep track of the information. The
census figures were then put into
electrical counting machines (below).

Hollerith also invented a machine to select special cards from the millions.

To find out how many people lived in Pennsylvania, the machine would select only the cards punched with a Pennsylvania hole.

Hollerith's punched cards made it possible to count and keep records on over 60 million people.

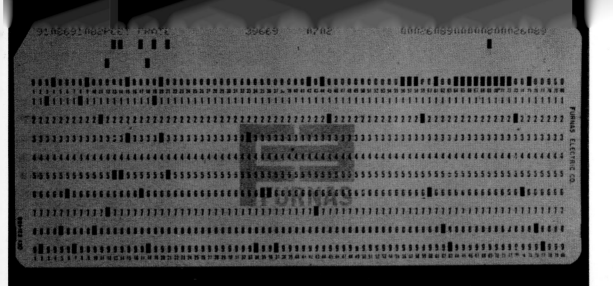

MODERN COMPUTERS

Since Hollerith's time, punch cards have been greatly improved.

Now they are 80 rows wide and 12 rows high.

There are 960 places to punch holes on each card.

A card reader can read hundreds of cards a minute.

After the cards are
punched, they are put into
a card reader machine.

The card reader feels
the placement of the holes
in each card. It sends the
information on the card
into the computer.

Left: Terminal
Above: Computer bank

Computers can receive "input" from holes punched in cards or paper tape, from computer keyboards, and from special magnetic tapes.

Information input is the first step in computer operation.

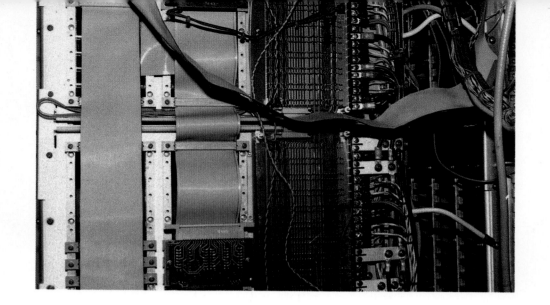

COMPUTER CODES

Inside a computer, information is changed into a special code. It is called THE BINARY NUMBER CODE.

The only symbols used to make binary code numbers are "1" and "0."

Although it may seem difficult to understand, the Binary Number Code is easy—once you see how it works.

The Binary Number Code is based on the idea of doubling the value of regular numbers:
1+1=2, 2+2=4, 4+4=8, and so on.

The doubled numbers are then arranged from right to left ... 8 4 2 1.

To write the code number for "1," put a 1 under the 1. Then write 0s under the 2, the 4, and the 8.

$$1 = \frac{8\ 4\ 2\ 1}{0\ 0\ 0\ 1}$$

To write the code number for "2," put a 1 under the 2. Then write 0s under the 1, the 4, and the 8.

$$2 = \frac{8\ 4\ 2\ 1}{0\ 0\ 1\ 0}$$

To write the code number for "3," put a
1 under the 2 and another 1 under the 1.
Then write 0s under the 4 and the 8.

$$2+1=3, \text{ so } 3 = \frac{8 \quad 4 \quad 2 \quad 1}{0 \quad 0 \quad 1 \quad 1}$$

To write "4," put a 1 under the 4. Then
write 0s under the 1, the 2, and the 8.

$$4 = \frac{8 \quad 4 \quad 2 \quad 1}{0 \quad 1 \quad 0 \quad 0}$$

To make a number in the Binary
Number Code you put the number 1
under the numbers that add up to that
number.

To write "5," put a 1 under the 4 and
another 1 under the 1. Then, write 0s
under the 2 and the 8.

$$4+1=5, \text{ so } 5 = \frac{8 \quad 4 \quad 2 \quad 1}{0 \quad 1 \quad 0 \quad 1}$$

Can you write the binary code numbers
for "6" through "15?" Look on page 46
and see if you wrote the numbers
30   correctly.

At "16," you need to add another place to the left.

$$8+8=16, \text{ so } 16 = \frac{16 \quad 8 \quad 4 \quad 2 \quad 1}{1 \quad 0 \quad 0 \quad 0 \quad 0}$$

With five places, you can write all the code numbers from "16" through "31." Look on page 46 and see if you wrote the numbers correctly.

At "32," add another place on the left.

$$16+16=32, \text{ so } 32 = \frac{32 \quad 16 \quad 8 \quad 4 \quad 2 \quad 1}{1 \quad 0 \quad 0 \quad 0 \quad 0 \quad 0}$$

At what number will you have to add another place to the left? If you said 64, you would be correct. Remember each time you add a place to the left you double the number of numbers you can represent.

Binary code numbers can go as high as the highest number that you can imagine.

Computers change regular numbers into code numbers. They also change letters of the alphabet into code numbers.

There are 26 letters in the alphabet, so each one needs its own code number.
"A" can equal "1" or 0001...
"B" can equal "2" or 0010...
"C" can equal "3" or 0011...
and so on to "Z" can equal "26" or 11010.

To show a difference between the code for numbers and the code for letters, add another code number for each. So,

1 = 011 0001   A = 100 0001
2 = 011 0010   B = 100 0010
3 = 011 0011   C = 100 0011
and so on.

A computer changes everything into code. It changes the code into electrical charges.

The 1s in the code receive a charge, and the 0s receive no charge.

The 1s are "on." The 0s are "off." So, 100 0011 becomes "on/off/off off/off/ on/on."

The computer sends these charges to its memory.

The memory in a large computer can store millions of numbers or an entire library of words.

COMPUTER PROGRAMS

Computers follow definite instructions.

Computer instructions are called "programs."

A program tells a computer what to do.

The program tells the computer to find certain information in its memory.

Then it tells the computer to send the information over to its arithmetic unit. This unit can do addition, subtraction, multiplication, division, and other kinds of problem solving. It follows a program to its end.

The memory of a computer stores everything that comes into a computer.

Then it sends the final answer to the memory for storage and to the computer's terminal.

A computer terminal
reports what the computer
has been doing.
There are many kinds of
terminals.

Computer printout (below) and
computerized display terminal at
an airport (right).

SKED DEPART	DEPARTING TO	WILL DEPART	FLT	GATE
2:35	NEWARK	2:35	142	F5
3:00	WASHINGTON-NATIONAL	CANCLD	332	
3:35	AKRON/CANTON	CANCLD	616	
3:40	HOUSTON	3:40	301	E2
3:40	ONTARIO	CANCLD	889	
3:40	SACRAMENTO/PORTLAND	CANCLD	669	
3:40	PHOENIX	CANCLD	209	
3:45	MINNEAPOLIS/ST. PAUL	3:45	603	F4
3:45	SAN FRANCISCO	3:45	129	F3
3:45	SANTA BARBARA	CANCLD	697	
3:45	OAKLAND/SAN FRANCISCO	3:45	917	E8
3:45	DENVER	3:45	205	E5
3:45	VANCOUVER	3:45	201	F11
3:45	SEATTLE/TACOMA	3:45	155	E11
3:45	LOS ANGELES	3:45	111	E3

TUESDAY 1:47:24

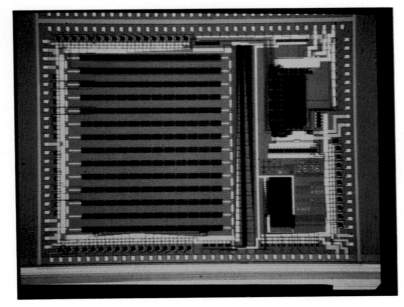

This is a microchip. It is as small as, or smaller, than your fingernail.

MICROCHIPS AND MICROCOMPUTERS

Computers are always being changed and improved.

A recent improvement is the microchip.

Microchips can store electrical charges. Each one can hold thousands of pieces of memory information.

Microchips are easy to make, strong, and very inexpensive.

Microchips are used in

- computer games
- microwave ovens
- microcomputers

Microcomputers are
small computers. They are
much less expensive than
earlier computers.

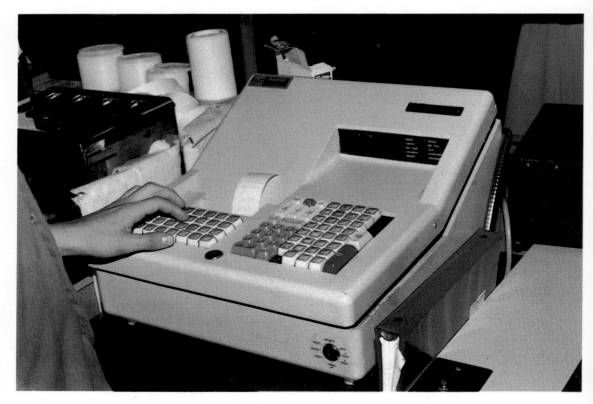

Computerized cash register

In stores and businesses, computers keep track of many things. They can even print out bills to send to customers.

In schools, computers help students to learn new facts and new ways to do things.

In a hospital, a computer can have many uses.

Intensive care unit's heart monitors

Computers at Johnson Space Center

Without computers, there would be no space flights. There are just too many problems to solve.

Scientists can do all the arithmetic, but they are too slow. Computers can do the work much faster.

Computers can remember everything. They can follow the same program, over and over, without getting bored.

Computers are wonderful machines, right now. In the future computers will be even better.

Binary Number Code from 6 through 15			
	8	4	2	1

	8	4	2	1
6	0	1	1	0
7	0	1	1	1
8	1	0	0	0
9	1	0	0	1
10	1	0	1	0
11	1	0	1	1
12	1	1	0	0
13	1	1	0	1
14	1	1	1	0
15	1	1	1	1

Binary Number Code from 17 through 31

	16	8	4	2	1
17	1	0	0	0	1
18	1	0	0	1	0
19	1	0	0	1	1
20	1	0	1	0	0
21	1	0	1	0	1
22	1	0	1	1	0
23	1	0	1	1	1
24	1	1	0	0	0
25	1	1	0	0	1
26	1	1	0	1	0
27	1	1	0	1	1
28	1	1	1	0	0
29	1	1	1	0	1
30	1	1	1	1	0
31	1	1	1	1	1

WORDS YOU SHOULD KNOW

abacus(AB • uh • kuss) — a hand-operated device used for counting, made up of a frame and beads

arithmetic unit(ah • RITH • meh • tik YOO • nit) — the part of a computer in which arithmetic problems are solved

arrange(ah • RAINJ) — to put in a certain order

Binary Number Code(BY • nairy NUM • ber COHDE) — a pattern of numbers, using only "1" and "0" in different combinations to stand for other numbers

circuit(SIR • kit) — the path that an electric current takes

code(COHDE) — a system of signals that stands for letters or numbers

community(kum • MYOON • ih • tee) — a place where people live together

complicated(KOM • plih • kay • ted) — not easy to understand

definite(DEF • in • it) — exact; specific; to be very clear

display — show

electric charge(ee • LEK • trik CHARJ) — to put electrical power into something

electric meter(ee • LEK • trik MEE • ter) — something that measures how much electricity is being used

entire(en • TYER) — everything; all

equal(EE • kwil) — to be the same as

grain — the seed of wheat, corn, rice, and other cereal plants

improve(im • PROOV) — to make better

input(IN • put) — information that is put into a computer

invent(in • VENT) — to think up and make something that did not exist before

keyboard(KEE • bord) — a set of keys on a typewriter

memory(MEM • ree) — the part of a computer where the information is stored

microchip(MY • kro • chip) — a very small part of a computer that helps make it run electrically

microcomputer(MY • kro • kom • PYOO • ter) — a small computer using microchips

monitor(MON • ih • ter) — to watch; to keep track of

notch — a v-shaped cut in something

program — a list of step-by-step instructions that tells a computer how to solve a problem

punctuation(PUNK • chu • A • shun) — the use of periods, commas, and other marks that helps make writing material clear

repeat(ree • PEET) — to do or say again

replace — to take the place of; to put in another

reverse — to turn around; backward

select(sih • LECT) — to pick; choose

solution(suh • LOO • shun) — answer

surround(sir • rownd) — to be on all sides of; to encircle

terminal(TER • min • el) — the part of a computer where information comes out. It can be a keyboard, television screen, or recording.

trade(TRAYD) — to exchange; swap

weaving loom(WEE • ving LOOM) — a device on which cloth is made

worth(WERTH) — to have value

INDEX

About the Author

Karen Jacobsen is a graduate of the University of Connecticut and Syracuse University. She has been a teacher and is a writer. She likes to find out about interesting subjects and then write about them.